20. Tue. Tuesday of the 2nd Week in Ordinary Time
ALL 869, Rd & Pr 86; NP 1278

OR: St. Fabian, Po & M (1306)
From Com of M 1707 or Pas 1734
OOR 870, Rd 86 & 1306, Pr 1308
MP from Com, Ps 875, Pr 1308; DP 881
EP from Com, Ps 886, Pr 1308; NP 1278

OR: St. Sebastian, M (1308)
From Com of M 1707
OOR 870, Rd 86 & 1308, Pr 1310
MP 1715, Ps 875, Pr 1310; DP 881
EP 1721, Ps 886, Pr 1310; NP 1278

21. Wed. St. Agnes, V & M (Mem) (1310)
From Com of M 1707 or V 1777
OOR 892, Rd 90 & 1310, Pr 1313
MP 1312, Ps 688, Intercessions from Com; DP 903
EP 1314, Ps 1722, Intercessions from Com; NP 1280

22. Thu. Day of Prayer for the Legal Protection of Unborn Children
ALL 916, Rd & Pr 94; NP 1283

23. Fri. Friday of the 2nd Week in Ordinary Time
ALL 937, Rd & Pr 98; NP 1285

OR: St. Vincent, De & M (1315) **[transferred from 1/22]**
From Com of M 1707
OOR 938, Rd 98 & 1315, Pr 1317
MP 1715, Ps 941, Pr 1317; DP 947
EP 1721, Ps 952, Pr 1317; NP 1285

OR: St. Marianne Cope, V *(New)*
From Com of V 1777 or HW (Underpriv) 1866
OOR 938, Rd 98 & 1780 or 1866, Pr 1789
MP 1786, Ps 941, Pr 1789; DP 947
EP 1791, Ps 952, Pr 1789; NP 1285

24. Sat. St. Francis de Sales, B & D (Mem) (1317)
From Com of Pas 1734 or D 1763
OOR 959, Rd 103 & 1317, Pr 1319
MP from Com, Ps 962, Pr 1319; DP 968
EP I (of Sunday) 973, Ant & Pr 108; NP 1269

25. **Sun. THIRD SUNDAY IN ORDINARY TIME**
ALL 978, Rd, Te Deum, Ant & Pr 108; NP 1272

26. Mon. Sts. Timothy & Titus, Bb (Mem) (1329)
From Com of Pas 1734
OOR 998, Rd 113 & 1329, Pr 1331
MP 1749, Ps 1002, Ant & Pr 1331; DP 1007
EP 1755, Ps 1012, Ant 1332, Pr 1331; NP 1275

27. Tue. Tuesday of the 3rd Week in Ordinary Time
ALL 1018, Rd & Pr 118; NP 1278

OR: St. Angela Merici, V (1332)
From Com of V 1777 or Tea 1871
OOR 1019, Rd 118 & 1332, Pr 1334
MP from Com, Ps 1024, Pr 1334; DP 1029
EP from Com, Ps 1034, Pr 1334; NP 1278

28. Wed. St. Thomas Aquinas, P & D (Mem) (1334)
From Com of D 1763
OOR 1040, Rd 122 & 1335, Pr 1337
MP 1768, Ps 1045, Ant & Pr 1336; DP 1050
EP 1770, Ps 1056, Ant & Pr 1337; NP 1280

29. Thu. Thursday of the 3rd Week in Ordinary Time
ALL 1061, Rd & Pr 127; NP 1283

30. Fri. Friday of the 3rd Week in Ordinary Time
ALL 1082, Rd & Pr 131; NP 1285

31. Sat. St. John Bosco, P (Mem) (1337)
From Com of Pas 1734 or Tea 1871
OOR 1103, Rd 135 & 1337, Pr 1339
MP from Com, Ps 1108, Pr 1339; DP 1112
EP I (of Sunday) 1117, Ant & Pr 140; NP 1269

FEBRUARY

1. **Sun. FOURTH SUNDAY IN ORDINARY TIME**
ALL 1122, Rd, Te Deum, Ant & Pr 140; NP 1272

2. Mon. PRESENTATION OF THE LORD (F)
ALL 1345, Te Deum, DP Ps 1154; EP 1355; NP 1275

3. Tue. Tuesday of the 4th Week in Ordinary Time
ALL 1165, Rd & Pr 149; NP 1278

Saint Joseph

GUIDE

FOR

THE LITURGY OF THE HOURS

For 2015

No. 400/G

CATHOLIC BOOK PUBLISHING CORP.
New Jersey

www.catholicbookpublishing.com

The purpose of this handy Guide is to facilitate use of the **Liturgy of the Hours** by providing clear accurate references for each day of the period specified—always in accord with the principles set forth in the **General Instruction on the Liturgy of the Hours.**

Included with the **Liturgy of the Hours** is a card with an outline of the Hours and a Format of the Office. Until you become familiar with the present Divine Office, it might be necessary for you to refer to this card in conjunction with the references given in this GUIDE.

The designation **(New)** indicates that the Saint in question is found in the revised **SUPPLEMENT of the Liturgy of the Hours** (No. 405/04) published in 1992. (No **SUPPLEMENT** has been approved for publication since that time.) [The designation (*New*) in lightface italics indicates that the Saint in question must be taken from the pertinent Common.]

LIST OF ABBREVIATIONS

Ab — Abbot
ALL — All hours
Ant — Antiphon
Ap — Apostle
B, Bb — Bishop(s)
Bl. — Blessed
BVM — Blessed Virgin Mary
Com — Common
Comp(s) — Companion(s)
D, Dd — Doctor(s)
De — Deacon
Ded — Dedication of Church
DP — Daytime Prayer
EP — Evening Prayer
F — Feast
f — following page(s)
HM — Holy Men
HW — Holy Women
Invit — Invitatory
Mag — Magnificat, canticle of Mary
M, Mm — Martyr(s)
Mem — Memorial (Obligatory)
MP — Morning Prayer
NP — Night Prayer
OOR — Office of Readings
P, Pp — Priest(s)
Pas — Pastor
Po — Pope
Pr — Prayer
Ps — Psalmody
Rd — Reading(s)
Rel — Religious
Sol — Solemnity
St., Sts. — Saint(s)
Tea — Teacher
(Underpriv) — Those who work for underprivileged
V — Virgin

(400/G)

Printed in the U.S.A.
www.catholicbookpublishing.com

BEGIN WITH VOLUME I

JANUARY

1. **Thu. MARY, MOTHER OF GOD (Sol)**
ALL 479, Te Deum; DP Ps 1191; NP 1172
Hymns for Christmas Season, p. 385 and following.

2. Fri. Sts. Basil the Great & Gregory Nazianzen, Bb & Dd (Mem) (1285)
From Com of Pas 1428 or D 1458
OOR from Com, Ps 765, Rd 533 & 1285, Pr 1287
MP from Com, Ps 769, Ant & Pr 1287; DP 773, Ant, Rd, etc. 536
EP from Com, Ps 777, Ant & Pr 1288; NP 1185

3. Sat. Saturday before Epiphany or The Most Holy Name of Jesus (*New*) No official texts yet exist in English.
ALL 781, Ant, Rd, etc. 539
EP I (of Epiphany) 546; NP 1169

4. **Sun. EPIPHANY (Sol)**
ALL 551, Te Deum; NP 1172
Hymns after Epiphany from the Feast or from Christmas Season, p. 385 and following.

5. Mon. St. John Neumann, B (Mem) (1692)
From Com of Pas 1428
OOR 1428, Ps 817, Rd 575 & 1692, Pr 1695
MP 1443, Ps 822, Pr 1695; DP 825, Ant, Rd, etc. 581
EP 1449, Ps 829, Pr 1695; NP 1175

6. Tue. Tuesday after Epiphany
ALL 833, Ant, Rd, etc. 584; NP 1178

OR: St. André Bessette, Rel (**New**) (5)
From of Com of HM 1500 or Rel 1554
OOR 1500 or 1554, Ps 834, Rd 584 & 1556, Pr (6) or 1559
MP from Com, Ps 839, Pr (6) or 1559; DP 844, Ant, Rd, etc. 589
EP from Com, Ps 847, Pr (6) or 1559; NP 1178

7. Wed. Wednesday after Epiphany
ALL 851, Ant, Rd, etc. 592; NP 1180

OR: St. Raymond of Penyafort, P (1288)
From Com of Pas 1428
OOR 1428, Ps 852, Rd 592 & 1288, Pr 1290

MP 1443, Ps 857, Pr 1290; DP 862, Ant, Rd, etc. 598
EP 1449, Ps 867, Pr 1290; NP 1180

8. Thu. Thursday after Epiphany
ALL 872, Ant, Rd, etc. 601; NP 1183

9. Fri. Friday after Epiphany
ALL 890, Ant, Rd, etc. 609; NP 1185

10. Sat. Saturday after Epiphany
ALL 906, Ant, Rd, etc. 618
EP I (of Baptism) 625; NP 1169

11. **Sun. BAPTISM OF THE LORD (F)**
ALL 628, Te Deum; DP Ps 934; NP 1172

BEGIN VOLUME III

12. Mon. Monday of the 1st Week in Ordinary Time
ALL 702, Rd & Pr 53; NP 1275

13. Tue. Tuesday of the 1st Week in Ordinary Time
ALL 722, Rd & Pr 57; NP 1278

OR: St. Hilary, B & D (1301)
From Com of Pas 1734 or D 1763
OOR 723, Rd 57 & 1301, Pr 1303
MP from Com, Ps 728, Pr 1303; DP 733
EP from Com, Ps 739, Pr 1303; NP 1278

14. Wed. Wednesday of the 1st Week in Ordinary Time
ALL 744, Rd & Pr 60; NP 1280

15. Thu. Thursday of the 1st Week in Ordinary Time
ALL 765, Rd & Pr 65; NP 1283

16. Fri. Friday of the 1st Week in Ordinary Time
ALL 786, Rd & Pr 69; NP 1285

17. Sat. St. Anthony, Ab (Mem) (1303)
From Com of Rel 1858
OOR 807, Rd 73 & 1304, Pr 1305
MP 1862, Ps 811, Pr 1305; DP 816
EP I (of Sunday) 821, Ant & Pr 78; NP 1269

18. **Sun. SECOND SUNDAY IN ORDINARY TIME**
ALL 826, Rd, Te Deum, Ant & Pr 78; NP 1272

19. Mon. Monday of the 2nd Week in Ordinary Time
ALL 847, Rd & Pr 82; NP 1275

OR: St. Blase, B & M (1360)
From Com of M 1707 or Pas 1734
OOR 1166, Rd 149 & 1360, Pr 1362
MP from Com, Ps 1170, Pr 1362; DP 1176
EP from Com, Ps 1180, Pr 1362; NP 1278

OR: St. Ansgar, B (1362)
From Com of Pas 1734
OOR 1166, Rd 149 & 1362, Pr 1364
MP 1749, Ps 1170, Pr 1364; DP 1176
EP 1755, Ps 1180, Pr 1364; NP 1278

4. Wed. Wednesday of the 4th Week in Ordinary Time
ALL 1187, Rd & Pr 152; NP 1280

5. Thu. St. Agatha, V & M (Mem) (1364)
From Com of M 1707 or V 1777
OOR 1211, Rd 156 & 1365, Pr 1366
MP from Com, Ps 1214, Ant & Pr 1366; DP 1219
EP from Com, Ps 1225, Ant & Pr 1367; NP 1283

6. Fri. St. Paul Miki & Comps, Mm (Mem) (1367)
From Com of Mm 1680
OOR 1231, Rd 160 & 1367, Pr 1369
MP 1688, Ps 1234, Pr 1369; DP 1240
EP 1694, Ps 1246, Pr 1369; NP 1285

7. Sat. Saturday of the 4th Week in Ordinary Time
ALL 1250, Rd & Pr 164; EP see below

OR: BVM on Saturday—1642 & 1251
Rd 164 & 1642f, Pr 1653f; DP 1259
EP I (of Sunday) 677, Ant & Pr 168; NP 1269

8. **Sun. FIFTH SUNDAY IN ORDINARY TIME**
ALL 682, Rd, Te Deum, Ant & Pr 168; NP 1272

9. Mon. Monday of the 5th Week in Ordinary Time
ALL 702, Rd & Pr 172; NP 1275

10. Tue. St. Scholastica, V (Mem) (1372)
From Com of V 1777
OOR 723, Rd 176 & 1372, Pr 1374
MP 1786, Ps 728; Ant & Pr 1374; DP 733
EP 1791, Ps 739, Pr 1374; NP 1278

11. Wed. Wednesday of the 5th Week in Ordinary Time
ALL 744, Rd & Pr 181; NP 1280

OR: Our Lady of Lourdes (1374)
From Com of BVM 1614
OOR 745, Rd 181 & 1375, Pr 1377
MP 1626, Ps 749, Ant & Pr 1377; DP 754
EP 1634, Ps 759, Ant & Pr 1377; NP 1280

12. Thu. Thursday of the 5th Week in Ordinary Time
ALL 765, Rd & Pr 185; NP 1283

13. Fri. Friday of the 5th Week in Ordinary Time
ALL 786, Rd & Pr 189; NP 1285

14. Sat. Sts. Cyril, Monk & Methodius, B (Mem) (1377)
From Com of Pas 1734
OOR 807, Rd 193 & 1378, Pr 1380
MP 1749, Ps 811, Ant & Pr 1379; DP 816
EP I (of Sunday) 821, Ant & Pr 197; NP 1269

15. **Sun. SIXTH SUNDAY IN ORDINARY TIME**
ALL 826, Rd, Te Deum, Ant & Pr 197; NP 1272

16. Mon. Monday of the 6th Week in Ordinary Time
ALL 847, Rd & Pr 201; NP 1275

17. Tue. Tuesday of the 6th Week in Ordinary Time
ALL 869, Rd & Pr 205; NP 1278

OR: Seven Founders of the Order of Servites (1380)
From Com of Rel 1858
OOR 869, Rd 205 & 1380, Pr 1383
MP 1862, Ps 875, Ant 1382, Pr 1383; DP 881
EP 1864, Ps 886, Pr 1383; NP 1278

BEGIN VOLUME II

Hymns for Lenten Season before Holy Week: 33-47

18. Wed. Ash Wednesday
ALL 49, Ps 1551; NP 1638, Hymn 38

19. Thu. Thursday after Ash Wednesday
ALL 58, Ps 1571; NP 1642

20. Fri. Friday after Ash Wednesday
ALL 66, Ps 1588; NP 1644

21. Sat. Saturday after Ash Wednesday
OOR 75, Ps 1607 (May add Rd & Pr of St. Peter Damian, B & D 1681-1684)
MP 79, Ps 1610 (May add Ant & Pr of St. Peter Damian 1683)
DP 80, Ps 1615
EP I (of Sunday) 82, Ps 1076; NP 1625
22. **Sun. FIRST SUNDAY OF LENT**
ALL 84, Ps 1082; NP 1628, Hymn 38
23. Mon. Monday of the 1st Week of Lent
OOR 94, Ps 1102 (May add Rd & Pr of St. Polycarp, B & M 1694-1697)
MP 98, Ps 1107 (May add Ant & Pr of St. Polycarp 1697)
DP 99, Ps 1111
EP 100, Ps 1115 (May add Ant & Pr of St. Polycarp 1697)
NP 1632
24. Tue. Tuesday of the 1st Week of Lent
ALL 102, Ps 1121; NP 1635
25. Wed. Wednesday of the 1st Week of Lent
ALL 111, Ps 1141; NP 1638
26. Thu. Thursday of the 1st Week of Lent
ALL 120, Ps 1158; NP 1642
27. Fri. Friday of the 1st Week of Lent
ALL 129, Ps 1176; NP 1644
28. Sat. Saturday of the 1st Week of Lent
ALL 137, Ps 1194
EP I (of Sunday) 145, Ps 1208; NP 1625

MARCH

1. **Sun. SECOND SUNDAY OF LENT**
ALL 147, Ps 1214; NP 1628
2. Mon. Monday of the 2nd Week of Lent
ALL 157, Ps 1236; NP 1632
3. Tue. Tuesday of the 2nd Week of Lent
OOR 166, Ps 1257 (May add Rd & Pr of St. Katharine Drexel, V [**New**] Rd 2110, Pr [7] or 2118)
MP 170, Ps 1263 (May add Ant & Pr [7] of St. Katharine Drexel 2117)
DP 172, Ps 1268

EP 173, Ps 1272 (May add Ant & Pr [7] of St. Katharine Drexel 2125); NP 1635

4. Wed. Wednesday of the 2nd Week of Lent
OOR 175, Ps 1278 (May add Rd & Pr of St. Casimir 1698-1700)
MP 179, Ps 1284 (May add Ant & Pr of St. Casimir 1700)
DP 181, Ps 1290
EP 182, Ps 1295 (May add Ant & Pr of St. Casimir 1700)
NP 1638

5. Thu. Thursday of the 2nd Week of Lent
ALL 184, Ps 1302; NP 1642

6. Fri. Friday of the 2nd Week of Lent
ALL 192, Ps 1322; NP 1644

7. Sat. Saturday of the 2nd Week of Lent
OOR 201, Ps 1340 (May add Rd & Pr of Sts. Perpetua & Felicity, Mm 1701-1703)
MP 205, Ps 1345 (May add Ant & Pr of Sts. Perpetua & Felicity 1703)
DP 206, Ps 1350
EP I (of Sunday) 208, Ps 1355; NP 1625

8. **Sun. THIRD SUNDAY OF LENT**
ALL 210, Ps 1360; NP 1628

9. Mon. Monday of the 3rd Week of Lent
OOR 221, Ps 1379 (May add Rd & Pr of St. Frances of Rome, Rel 1707-1709)
MP 224, Ps 1383 (May add Ant & Pr of St. Frances of Rome 1709)
DP 226, Ps 1388
EP 227, Ps 1392 (May add Ant & Pr of St. Frances of Rome 1709)
NP 1632

10. Tue. Tuesday of the 3rd Week of Lent
ALL 228, Ps 1397; NP 1635

11. Wed. Wednesday of the 3rd Week of Lent
ALL 237, Ps 1416; NP 1638

12. Thu. Thursday of the 3rd Week of Lent
ALL 246, Ps 1435; NP 1642

13. Fri. Friday of the 3rd Week of Lent
ALL 256, Ps 1454; NP 1644

14. Sat. Saturday of the 3rd Week of Lent
ALL 263, Ps 1472
EP I (of Sunday) 271, Ps 1486; NP 1625

15. **Sun. FOURTH SUNDAY OF LENT**
ALL 273, Ps 1491; NP 1628

16. Mon. Monday of the 4th Week of Lent
ALL 283, Ps 1512; NP 1632

17. Tue. Tuesday of the 4th Week of Lent
OOR 292, Ps 1532 (May add Rd & Pr of St. Patrick, B 1710-1712)
MP 297, Ps 1537 (May add Ant & Pr of St. Patrick 1712);
DP 298, Ps 1541
EP 299, Ps 1545 (May add Ant & Pr of St. Patrick 1712); NP 1635

18. Wed. Wednesday of the 4th Week of Lent
OOR 301, Ps 1551 (May add Rd & Pr of St. Cyril of Jerusalem, B & D 1713-1715)
MP 306, Ps 1556 (May add Ant & Pr of St. Cyril of Jerusalem 1715)
DP 308, Ps 1560
EP I (of St. Joseph) 1716; NP 1625

19. Thu. ST. JOSEPH, HUSBAND OF MARY (Sol)
ALL 1719, Te Deum; DP Ps 1651; NP 1628

20. Fri. Friday of the 4th Week of Lent
ALL 320, Ps 1588; NP 1644

21. Sat. Saturday of the 4th Week of Lent
ALL 328, Ps 1607
EP I (of Sunday) 336, Ps 1076; NP 1625

22. **Sun. FIFTH SUNDAY OF LENT**
ALL 338, Ps 1082; NP 1628

23. Mon. Monday of the 5th Week of Lent
OOR 348, Ps 1102 (May add Rd & Pr of St. Turibius de Mogrovejo, B 1730-1732)
MP 352, Ps 1107 (May add Ant & Pr of St. Turibius 1732)
DP 354, Ps 1111
EP 355, Ps 1115 (May add Ant & Pr of St. Turibius 1732)
NP 1632

24. Tue. Tuesday of the 5th Week of Lent
ALL 356, Ps 1121
EP I (of Annunciation) 1733; NP 1625

25. Wed. ANNUNCIATION OF THE LORD (Sol)
ALL 1738, Te Deum; DP Ps 1651; NP 1628
26. Thu. Thursday of the 5th Week of Lent
ALL 373, Ps 1158; NP 1642
27. Fri. Friday of the 5th Week of Lent
ALL 381, Ps 1176; NP 1644
28. Sat. Saturday of the 5th Week of Lent
ALL 390, Ps 1194
EP I (of Sunday) 413, Ps 1208; NP 1625
Hymns during Holy Week 398-412
29. **Sun. PASSION SUNDAY (PALM SUNDAY)**
ALL 416, Ps 1214; NP 1628
30. Mon. Monday of Holy Week
ALL 430, Hymn 403; Ps 1236; NP 1632
31. Tue. Tuesday of Holy Week
ALL 439, Hymn 403; Ps 1257; NP 1635

APRIL

1. Wed. Wednesday of Holy Week
ALL 447, Hymn 403; Ps 1278; NP 1638
2. Thu. HOLY THURSDAY
OOR 457, Hymn 403; Ps 1302 or 1454
MP 460, Hymn 408; Ps 1306; DP 462, Ps 1311
EP (if absent from Lord's Supper) 464, Ps 1316
NP 1628, proper Ant instead of Responsory
3. Fri. GOOD FRIDAY
ALL 467
EP (if absent from Lord's Passion) 487
NP 1628, proper Ant instead of Responsory
4. Sat. HOLY SATURDAY
ALL 492; EP 509
NP (if absent from Easter Vigil) 1628, proper Ant
Hymns for Easter Season 536-548
5. **Sun. EASTER SUNDAY**
OOR (if absent from Easter Vigil) 515, Te Deum
MP 524, Invitatory, Ps 1088; DP 526, Hymn 546

EP 531, Hymn 536
NP 1625 or 1628, Hymn 540, Ant instead of Responsory 541

6. Mon. MONDAY WITHIN THE OCTAVE OF EASTER
OOR 549, Te Deum; MP 556, Hymn, etc. 524
DP 557, Hymn 546; EP 561, Hymn, etc. 531
NP 1625 or 1628, Hymn 540, Ant instead of Responsory 541

7. Tue. TUESDAY WITHIN THE OCTAVE OF EASTER
OOR 563, Te Deum; MP 570, Hymn, etc. 524
DP 571, Hymn 546; EP 575, Hymn, etc. 531
NP 1625 or 1628, Hymn 540, Ant instead of Responsory 541

8. Wed. WEDNESDAY WITHIN THE OCTAVE OF EASTER
OOR 577, Te Deum; MP 584, Hymn, etc. 524
DP 586, Hymn 546; EP 589, Hymn, etc. 531
NP 1625 or 1628, Hymn 540, Ant instead of Responsory 541

9. Thu. THURSDAY WITHIN THE OCTAVE OF EASTER
OOR 591, Te Deum; MP 598, Hymn, etc. 524
DP 599, Hymn 546; EP 603, Hymn, etc. 531
NP 1625 or 1628, Hymn 540, Ant instead of Responsory 541

10. Fri. FRIDAY WITHIN THE OCTAVE OF EASTER
OOR 604, Te Deum; MP 610, Hymn, etc. 524
DP 612, Hymn 546; EP 615, Hymn, etc. 531
NP 1625 or 1628, Hymn 540, Ant instead of Responsory 541

11. Sat. SATURDAY WITHIN THE OCTAVE OF EASTER
OOR 617, Te Deum
MP 623, Hymn, etc. 524; DP 624, Hymn 546
EP I (of Sunday) 629, Hymn, etc. 531
NP 1625 or 1628, Hymn 540, Ant instead of Responsory 541

12. **Sun. SECOND SUNDAY OF EASTER**
OOR 631, Te Deum
MP 637, Hymn, etc. 524; DP 526, Pr 638
EP 639, Hymn, etc. 531; NP 1628

13. Mon. Monday of the 2nd Week of Easter
ALL 642, Hymn 542, Ps 1236
MP 646, Hymn 544, Ps 1241; DP 647, Hymn 546, Ps 1247
EP 649, Hymn 536, Ps 1250; NP 1632, Hymn 540

OR: St. Martin I, Po & M (1770)
From Com of M in Easter 2015 or Pas 2052

OOR 1236, Rd 642 & 1771, Pr 1773
MP from Com, Ps 1241, Pr 1773; DP 648, Ps 1247
EP from Com, Ps 1251, Pr 1773; NP 1632

14. Tue. Tuesday of the 2nd Week of Easter
OOR 650, Hymn 542, Ps 1257
MP 654, Hymn 544, Ps 1263; DP 655, Hymn 546, Ps 1268
EP 656, Hymn 536, Ps 1272; NP 1635, Hymn 540

15. Wed. Wednesday of the 2nd Week of Easter
ALL 658, Ps 1278; NP 1638

16. Thu. Thursday of the 2nd Week of Easter
ALL 666, Ps 1302; NP 1642

17. Fri. Friday of the 2nd Week of Easter
ALL 675, Ps 1322; NP 1644

18. Sat. Saturday of the 2nd Week of Easter
ALL 683, Ps 1340
EP I (of Sunday) 690, Ps 1355; NP 1625

19. **Sun. THIRD SUNDAY OF EASTER**
ALL 692, Ps 1360, Te Deum; NP 1628

20. Mon. Monday of the 3rd Week of Easter
ALL 702, Ps 1379; NP 1632

21. Tue. Tuesday of the 3rd Week of Easter
ALL 710, Ps 1397; NP 1635

OR: St. Anselm, B & D (1773)
From Com of Pas 2052 or D 2086
OOR 1397, Rd 710 & 1774, Pr 1776
MP from Com, Ps 1402, Pr 1776; DP 715, Ps 1407
EP from Com, Ps 1411, Pr 1776; NP 1635

22. Wed. Wednesday of the 3rd Week of Easter
ALL 718, Ps 1416; NP 1638

23. Thu. Thursday of the 3rd Week of Easter
ALL 726, Ps 1435; NP 1642

OR: St. George, M (1777)
From Com of M in Easter 2015
OOR 1435, Rd 726 & 1777, Pr 1779
MP 2024, Ps 1440, Pr 1779; DP 730, Ps 1445
EP 2035, Ps 1450, Pr 1779; NP 1642

OR: St. Adalbert, B & M (*New*)
From Com of M in Easter 2015 or Pas 2052
OOR 1435, Rd 726 & 2022 or 2064, Pr proper or 2028 or 2074
MP from Com, Ps 1440, Pr as above; DP 730, Ps 1445
EP from Com, Ps 1450, Pr as above; NP 1642

24. Fri. Friday of the 3rd Week of Easter
ALL 733, Ps 1454; NP 1644

OR: St. Fidelis of Sigmaringen, P & M (1779)
From Com of M in Easter 2015 or Pas 2052
OOR 1454, Rd 733 & 1780, Pr 1781
MP from Com, Ps 1459, Pr 1781; DP 738, Ps 1463
EP from Com, Ps 1468, Pr 1781; NP 1644

25. Sat. ST. MARK, EVANGELIST (F) (1782)
From Com of Ap in Easter 1951 and Proper; Te Deum
DP 1481, Rd, etc. 1788, Pr 1787
EP I (of Sunday) 748, Ps 1486; NP 1625

26. **Sun. FOURTH SUNDAY OF EASTER**
ALL 750, Ps 1491, Te Deum; NP 1628

27. Mon. Monday of the 4th Week of Easter
ALL 760, Ps 1512; NP 1632

28. Tue. Tuesday of the 4th Week of Easter
ALL 768, Ps 1532; NP 1635

OR: St. Peter Chanel, P & M (1791)
From Com of M in Easter 2015
OOR 1532, Rd 768 & 1791, Pr 1793
MP 2024, Ps 1537, Pr 1793; DP 774, Ps 1541
EP 2035, Ps 1545, Pr 1793; NP 1635

OR: St. Louis Grignion de Montfort, P (*New* or Com)
From Com of Pas 2052
OOR 1532, Rd 768 & 2059, Pr 2075 (*New* or Com)
MP 2070, Ps 1537, Pr as above; DP 774, Ps 1541
EP 2077, Ps 1545, Pr as above; NP 1635

29. Wed. St. Catherine of Siena, V & D (Mem) (1793)
From Com of V 2104
OOR 1551, Rd 777 & 1794, Pr 1796
MP 2114, Ps 1556, Ant & Pr 1796; DP 782, Ps 1560
EP 2120, Ps 1565, Ant & Pr 1796; NP 1638

30. Thu. Thursday of the 4th Week of Easter
ALL 785, Ps 1571; NP 1642

OR: St. Pius, V Po (1796)
From Com of Pas 2052
OOR 1571, Rd 785 & 1796, Pr 1798
MP 2070, Ps 1574, Pr 1798; DP 791, Ps 1579
EP 2077, Ps 1583, Pr 1798; NP 1642

MAY

1. Fri. Friday of the 4th Week of Easter
ALL 794, Ps 1588; NP 1644

OR: St. Joseph the Worker (1800)
OOR 1800, Ps 1588, Rd 794 & 1800, Pr 1805
MP 1803, Ps 1593, Pr 1805; DP 800, Ps 1598
EP 1805, Ps 1601, Pr 1805; NP 1644

2. Sat. St. Athanasius, B & D (Mem) (1807)
From Com of Pas 2052 or D 2086
OOR 1607, Rd 803 & 1808, Pr 1810
MP from Com 2070, Ps 1611, Pr 1810; DP 809, Ps 1615
EP I (of Sunday) 811, Ps 1076, NP 1625

3. **Sun. FIFTH SUNDAY OF EASTER**
ALL 813, Ps 1082, Te Deum; NP 1628

4. Mon. Monday of the 5th Week of Easter
ALL 823, Ps 1102; NP 1632

5. Tue. Tuesday of the 5th Week of Easter
ALL 831, Ps 1121; NP 1635

6. Wed. Wednesday of the 5th Week of Easter
ALL 839, Ps 1141; NP 1638

7. Thu. Thursday of the 5th Week of Easter
ALL 847, Ps 1158; NP 1642

8. Fri. Friday of the 5th Week of Easter
ALL 854, Ps 1176; NP 1644

9. Sat. Saturday of the 5th Week of Easter
ALL 862, Ps 1194
EP I (of Sunday) 869, Ps 1208; NP 1625

10. **Sun. SIXTH SUNDAY OF EASTER**
ALL 871, Ps 1214, Te Deum; NP 1628

11. Mon. Monday of the 6th Week of Easter
ALL 880, Ps 1236; NP 1632

12. Tue. Tuesday of the 6th Week of Easter
ALL 888, Ps 1257; NP 1635

OR: Sts. Nereus & Achilleus, Mm (1817)
From Com of Mm in Easter 1977
OOR 1257, Rd 888 & 1817, Pr 1819
MP 1987, Ps 1263, Pr 1819; DP 893, Ps 1268
EP 1997, Ps 1272, Pr 1819; NP 1635

OR: St. Pancras, M (1819)
From Com of M in Easter 2015
OOR 1257, Rd 888 & 1820, Pr 1821
MP 2024, Ps 1263, Pr 1821; DP 893, Ps 1268
EP 2035, Ps 1272, Pr 1821; NP 1635

13. Wed. Wednesday of the 6th Week of Easter
ALL 896, Ps 1278; EP see below

OR: Our Lady of Fatima (*New*)
OOR 1278, Rd 896 & 1924f, Pr 1937
MP 1934, Ps 1284, Pr 1937; DP 901, Ps 1290
EP I (of Ascension) 909; NP 1625

14. **Thu. ASCENSION OF THE LORD (Sol)** (holyday of obligation)
ALL 914, Te Deum; NP 1628

15. Fri. Friday of the 6th Week of Easter
ALL 935, Ps 1322; NP 1644

OR: St. Isidore (2341)
From Com of HM 2134
OOR 1322, Rd 935 or 2145, Pr 2341
MP 2149, Ps 1325, Pr 2341; DP 942, Ps 1330
EP 2157, Ps 1334, Pr 2341; NP 1644

16. Sat. Saturday of the 6th Week of Easter
ALL 946, Ps 1340
EP I (of Sunday) 954, Ps 1355; NP 1625

17. **Sun. SEVENTH SUNDAY OF EASTER**
ALL 956, Ps 1360, Te Deum; NP 1628

WHERE THE ASCENSION IS NOT TO BE OBSERVED AS A HOLYDAY OF OBLIGATION, IT IS ASSIGNED TO THE SEVENTH SUNDAY OF EASTER. **The specified rubrics below are to be followed until Monday of the 7th Week of Easter.**

13. Wed. Wednesday of the 6th Week of Easter
ALL 896, Ps 1278; EP 902; NP 1638

OR: Our Lady of Fatima (*New*)
OOR 1278, Rd 896 & 1924f, Pr 1937
MP 1934, Ps 1284, Pr 1937; DP 901, Ps 1290
EP 1939, Ps 1295, Pr 1937; NP 1638

14. Thu. Thursday of the 6th Week of Easter
OOR 904, Ps 1302, Verse, Rd & Resp 935 **(from Fri.)**; NP 1642

15. Fri. Friday of the 6th Week of Easter
ALL 935, Ps 1322, Verse, Rd & Resp 946 **(from Sat.)**; NP 1644

OR: St. Isidore (2341)
From Com of HM 2134
OOR 1322, Rd 935 or 2145, Pr 2341
MP 2149, Ps 1325, Pr 2341; DP 942, Ps 1330
EP 2157, Ps 1334, Pr 2341; NP 1644

16. Sat. Saturday of the 6th Week of Easter
ALL 946, Ps 1340, Verse, Rd & Resp 956 **(from Sun.)**
EP I (of Ascension) 909; NP 1625

17. **Sun. ASCENSION OF THE LORD (Sol)**
ALL 914, Te Deum; NP 1628

18. Mon. Monday of the 7th Week of Easter
ALL 965, Ps 1379; NP 1632

OR: St. John I, Po & M (1825)
From Com of M in Easter 2015 or Pas 2052
OOR 1379, Rd 965 & 1826, Pr 1828
MP from Com, Ps 1383, Pr 1828; DP 970, Ps 1388
EP from Com, Ps 1392, Pr 1828; NP 1632

19. Tue. Tuesday of the 7th Week of Easter
ALL 973, Ps 1397; NP 1635

20. Wed. Wednesday of the 7th Week of Easter
ALL 981, Ps 1416; NP 1638

OR: St. Bernardine of Siena, P (1828)
From Com of Pas 2052 or Rel 2195
OOR 1416, Rd 981 & 1828, Pr 1830
MP from Com, Ps 1421, Pr 1830; DP 986, Ps 1426
EP from Com, Ps 1430, Pr 1830; NP 1638

21. Thu. Thursday of the 7th Week of Easter
ALL 989, Ps 1435; NP 1642

OR: St. Christopher Magallanes, P & Comps, Mm (*New*)
From Com of Mm in Easter 1977
OOR 1435, Rd 989 & 1984, Pr 1991
MP 1987, Ps 1440, Pr 1991; DP 993, Ps 1445
EP 1997, Ps 1450, Pr 1991; NP 1642

22. Fri. Friday of the 7th Week of Easter
ALL 996, Ps 1454; NP 1644

OR: St. Rita of Cascia, Rel (*New*)
From Com of HW 2171
OOR 1454, Rd 996 & 2175f, Pr 2184
MP 2179, Ps 1459, Pr 2184; DP 1001, Ps 1463
EP 2186, Ps 1468, Pr 2184; NP 1644

23. Sat. Saturday of the 7th Week of Easter
ALL 1004, Ps 1472
EP I (of Pentecost) 1011; NP 1625

24. **Sun. PENTECOST (Sol)**
ALL 1017, Te Deum; NP 1628

RETURN TO VOLUME III

25. Mon. Monday of the 8th Week in Ordinary Time
ALL 1143, Rd & Pr 263; NP 1275

OR: Venerable Bede, P & D (1423)
From Com of D 1763 or Rel 1858
OOR 1143, Rd 263 & 1423, Pr 1425
MP from Com, Ps 1148, Pr 1425; DP 1154
EP from Com, Ps 1160, Pr 1425; NP 1275

OR: St. Gregory VII, Po (1426)
From Com of Pas 1734
OOR 1143, Rd 263 & 1426, Pr 1428
MP 1749, Ps 1148, Pr 1428; DP 1154
EP 1755, Ps 1160, Pr 1428; NP 1275

OR: St. Mary Magdalene de Pazzi, V (1428)
From Com of V 1777 or Rel 1858
OOR 1143, Rd 263 & 1428, Pr 1430
MP from Com, Ps 1148, Pr 1430; DP 1154
EP from Com, Ps 1160, Pr 1430; NP 1275

26. Tue. St. Philip de Neri, P (Mem) (1431)
From Com of Pas 1734 or Rel 1858
OOR 1165, Rd 266 & 1431, Pr 1433
MP from Com, Ps 1170, Pr 1433; DP 1176
EP from Com, Ps 1181, Pr 1433; NP 1278

27. Wed. Wednesday of the 8th Week in Ordinary Time
ALL 1187, Rd & Pr 271; NP 1280

OR: St. Augustine of Canterbury, B (1433)
From Com of Pas 1734
OOR 1188, Rd 271 & 1434, Pr 1435
MP 1749, Ps 1192, Pr 1435; DP 1197
EP 1755, Ps 1204, Pr 1435; NP 1280

28. Thu. Thursday of the 8th Week in Ordinary Time
ALL 1210, Rd & Pr 275; NP 1283

29. Fri. Friday of the 8th Week in Ordinary Time
ALL 1230, Rd & Pr 279; NP 1285

30. Sat. Saturday of the 8th Week in Ordinary Time
ALL 1250, Rd & Pr 283; EP see below

OR: BVM on Saturday—1642 & 1250
Rd 283 & 1642f, Pr 1653f; DP 1259
EP I (of Trinity) 573; NP 1269

31. **Sun. TRINITY SUNDAY (Sol)**
ALL 578, Te Deum; DP Ps 693; NP 1272

JUNE

1. Mon. St. Justin, M (Mem) (1447)
From Com of M 1707
OOR 702, Rd 293 & 1447, Pr 1450
MP 1715, Ps 706, Ant 1449, Pr 1450; DP 711
EP 1721, Ps 717, Pr 1450; NP 1275

2. Tue. Tuesday of the 9th Week in Ordinary Time
ALL 722, Rd & Pr 297; NP 1278

OR: Sts. Marcellinus & Peter, Mm (1450)
From Com of Mm 1680
OOR 723, Rd 297 & 1450, Pr 1452
MP 1688, Ps 728, Pr 1452; DP 733
EP 1694, Ps 739, Pr 1452; NP 1278

3. Wed. St. Charles Lwanga & Comps, Mm (Mem) (1453)
From Com of Mm 1680
OOR 745, Rd 301 & 1453, Pr 1455
MP 1688, Ps 749, Pr 1455; DP 754
EP 1694, Ps 759, Pr 1455; NP 1280

4. Thu. Thursday of the 9th Week in Ordinary Time
ALL 765, Rd & Pr 306; NP 1283

5. Fri. St. Boniface, B & M (Mem) (1455)
From Com of M 1707 or Pas 1734
OOR 786, Rd 310 & 1455, Pr 1457
MP from Com, Ps 790, Pr 1457; DP 796
EP from Com, Ps 802, Pr 1457; NP 1285

6. Sat. Saturday of the 9th Week in Ordinary Time
ALL 807, Rd & Pr 314; EP see below

OR: St. Norbert, B (1458)
From Com of Pas 1734
OOR 807, Rd 314 & 1458, Pr 1460
MP 1749, Ps 811, Pr 1460; DP 816
EP see below

OR: EVM on Saturday—1642 & 807
Rd 314 & 1642f, Pr 1653f; DP 816
EP I (of Corpus Christi) 597; NP 1269

7. **Sun. CORPUS CHRISTI (Sol)**
ALL 604, Te Deum; DP Ps 693; NP 1272

8. Mon. Monday of the 10th Week in Ordinary Time
ALL 847, Rd & Pr 322; NP 1275

9. Tue. Tuesday of the 10th Week in Ordinary Time
ALL 869, Rd & Pr 326; NP 1278

OR: St. Ephrem, De & D (1460)
From Com of D 1763
OOR 870, Rd 326 & 1460, Pr 1462
MP 1768, Ps 875, Pr 1462; DP 881
EP 1770, Ps 886, Pr 1462; NP 1278

10. Wed. Wednesday of the 10th Week in Ordinary Time
ALL 891, Rd & Pr 331; NP 1280

11. Thu. St. Barnabas, Ap (Mem) (1462)
From Com of Ap and proper; Invit 1463

OOR Hymn 1659, Ps 917, Rd 336 & 1463, Pr 1466
MP Hymn 1666, Ps 920, Rd, etc. 1465
DP 926, Rd, etc. 1467
EP (of Sacred Heart) 624; NP 1269

12. Fri. SACRED HEART (Sol)
ALL 629, Te Deum; DP Ps 1291; NP 1272

13. Sat. Saturday of the 10th Week in Ordinary Time
ALL 958, Rd & Pr 345; EP see below

OR: Immaculate Heart of BVM (1444)
From Com of BVM 1614
OOR 959, Rd 345 & 1444, Pr 1446
MP 1626, Ps 962, Ant & Pr 1446; DP 968
EP see below

OR: St. Anthony of Padua, P & D (1469)
From Com of Pas 1734 or D 1763 or Rel 1858
OOR 959, Rd 345 & 1470, Pr 1471
MP from Com, Ps 962, Pr 1471; DP 968
EP see below

OR: BVM on Saturday—1642 & 958
Rd 345 & 1642f, Pr 1653f; DP 968
EP I (of Sunday) 973, Ant & Pr 350; NP 1269

14. **Sun. ELEVENTH SUNDAY IN ORDINARY TIME**
ALL 978, Rd, Te Deum, Ant & Pr 350; NP 1272

15. Mon. Monday of the 11th Week in Ordinary Time
ALL 998, Rd & Pr 355; NP 1275

16. Tue. Tuesday of the 11th Week in Ordinary Time
ALL 1018, Rd & Pr 360; NP 1278

17. Wed. Wednesday of the 11th Week in Ordinary Time
ALL 1039, Rd & Pr 364; NP 1280

18. Thu. Thursday of the 11th Week in Ordinary Time
ALL 1061, Rd & Pr 369; NP 1283

19. Fri. Friday of the 11th Week in Ordinary Time
ALL 1082, Rd & Pr 373; NP 1285

OR: St. Romuald, Ab (1472)
From Com of Rel 1858
OOR 1082, Rd 373 & 1472, Pr 1474

MP 1862, Ps 1087, Pr 1474; DP 1092
EP 1864, Ps 1098, Pr 1474; NP 1285

20. Sat. Saturday of the 11th Week in Ordinary Time
ALL 1103, Rd & Pr 378; EP see below

OR: BVM on Saturday—1642 & 1103
Rd 378 & 1642f, Pr 1653f; DP 1112
EP I (of Sunday) 1117, Ant & Pr 384; NP 1269

21. **Sun. TWELFTH SUNDAY IN ORDINARY TIME**
ALL 1122, Rd, Te Deum, Ant & Pr 384; NP 1272

22. Mon. Monday of the 12th Week in Ordinary Time
ALL 1143, Rd & Pr 388; NP 1275

OR: St. Paulinus of Nola, B (1476)
From Com of Pas 1734
OOR 1144, Rd 388 & 1477, Pr 1479
MP 1749, Ps 1148, Pr 1479; DP 1154
EP 1755, Ps 1160, Pr 1479; NP 1275

OR: Sts. John Fisher, B & M & Thomas More, M (1479)
From Com of Mm 1680
OOR 1144, Rd 388 & 1479, Pr 1481
MP 1688, Ps 1148, Ant & Pr 1481; DP 1154
EP 1694, Ps 1160, Ant & Pr 1481; NP 1275

23. Tue. Tuesday of the 12th Week in Ordinary Time
ALL 1165, Rd & Pr 393
EP (of St. John the Baptist) 1482; NP 1269

24. Wed. BIRTH OF ST. JOHN THE BAPTIST (Sol)
ALL 1485, Te Deum; DP Ps 1291; NP 1272

25. Thu. Thursday of the 12th Week in Ordinary Time
ALL 1210, Rd & Pr 401; NP 1283

26. Fri. Friday of the 12th Week in Ordinary Time
ALL 1230, Rd & Pr 405; NP 1285

27. Sat. Saturday of the 12th Week in Ordinary Time
ALL 1250, Rd & Pr 410; EP see below

OR: St. Cyril of Alexandria, B & D (1495)
From Com of Pas 1734 or D 1763
OOR 1251, Rd 410 & 1496, Pr 1497
MP from Com, Ps 1254, Pr 1497; DP 1259
EP see below

OR: BVM on Saturday—1642 & 1250
Rd 410 & 1642f, Pr 1653f; DP 1259
EP I (of Sunday) 677, Ant & Pr 415; NP 1269

28. **Sun. THIRTEENTH SUNDAY IN ORDINARY TIME**
ALL 682, Rd, Te Deum, Ant & Pr 415
EP I (of Sts. Peter & Paul) 1500; NP 1269

29. Mon. STS. PETER & PAUL, AP (Sol)
ALL 1503, Te Deum; DP 1291; NP 1272

30. Tue. Tuesday of the 13th Week in Ordinary Time
ALL 722, Rd & Pr 425; NP 1278

OR: First Martyrs of the Church of Rome (1513)
From Com of Mm 1680
OOR 723, Rd 425 & 1513, Pr 1515
MP 1688, Ps 728, Ant & Pr 1515; DP 733
EP 1694, Ps 739, Ant & Pr 1515; NP 1278

JULY

1. Wed. Wednesday of the 13th Week in Ordinary Time
ALL 744, Rd & Pr 429; NP 1280

OR: Bl. Junipero Serra, P (**New**) (8)
From Com of Pas 1734
OOR 745, Rd 429 or 1745, Pr proper (8) or 1753
MP 1749, Ps 749, Pr (8); DP 754
EP 1755, Ps 759, Pr (8); NP 1280

2. Thu. Thursday of the 13th Week in Ordinary Time
ALL 765, Rd & Pr 433; NP 1283

3. Fri. ST. THOMAS, AP (F) (1516)
From Com of Ap 1659 and proper, Te Deum
DP 796, Rd, etc. 1668, Pr 1519; NP 1285

4. Sat. Saturday of the 13th Week in Ordinary Time
ALL 807, Rd & Pr 442; EP see below

OR: BVM on Saturday—1642 & 807
Rd 442 & 1642f, Pr 1653f; DP 816
EP I (of Sunday) 821, Ant & Pr 447; NP 1269

5. **Sun. FOURTEENTH SUNDAY IN ORDINARY TIME**
ALL 826, Rd, Te Deum, Ant & Pr 447; NP 1272

6. Mon. Monday of the 14th Week in Ordinary Time
ALL 847, Rd & Pr 453; NP 1275

OR: St. Maria Goretti, V & M (1525)
From Com of M 1707 or V 1777
OOR 848, Rd 453 & 1525, Pr 1527
MP from Com, Ps 853, Pr 1527; DP 858
EP from Com, Ps 864, Pr 1527; NP 1275

7. Tue. Tuesday of the 14th Week in Ordinary Time
ALL 869, Rd & Pr 457; NP 1278

8. Wed. Wednesday of the 14th Week in Ordinary Time
ALL 891, Rd & Pr 462; NP 1280

9. Thu. Thursday of the 14th Week in Ordinary Time
ALL 916, Rd & Pr 467; NP 1283

OR: St. Augustine Zhao Rong, P & Comps, Mm (*New*)
From Com of Mm 1680
OOR 917, Rd 467 & 1686, Pr 1692
MP 1688, Ps 920, Ant & Pr 1691; DP 926
EP 1694, Ps 932, Ant & Pr 1698; NP 1283

10. Fri. Friday of the 14th Week in Ordinary Time
ALL 937, Rd & Pr 471; NP 1285

11. Sat. St. Benedict, Ab (Mem) (1527)
From Com of Rel 1858
OOR 959, Rd 475 & 1528, Pr 1530
MP 1862, Ps 962, Ant & Pr 1530; DP 968
EP I (of Sunday) 973, Ant & Pr 480; NP 1269

12. **Sun. FIFTEENTH SUNDAY IN ORDINARY TIME**
ALL 978, Rd, Te Deum, Ant & Pr 480; NP 1272

13. Mon. Monday of the 15th Week in Ordinary Time
ALL 998, Rd & Pr 485; NP 1275

OR: St. Henry (1531)
From Com of HM 1804
OCR 998, Rd 485 & 1531; Pr 1533
MP 1815, Ps 1002, Pr 1533; DP 1007
EP 1822, Ps 1012, Pr 1533; NP 1275

14. Tue. St. Kateri Tekakwitha, V (Mem) (**New**) (9)
From Com of V 1777
OOR 1019, Rd 489 & 1782, Pr proper (9) or 1789

MP 1786, Ps 1024, Pr proper (9) or 1789; DP 1029
EP 1791, Ps 1034, Pr proper (9) or 1789; NP 1278

15. Wed. St. Bonaventure, B & D (Mem) (1535)
From Com of Pas 1734 or D 1763
OOR 1040, Rd 494 & 1535, Pr 1537
MP from Com, Ps 1045, Pr 1537; DP 1050
EP from Com, Ps 1056, Pr 1537; NP 1280

16. Thu. Thursday of the 15th Week in Ordinary Time
ALL 1061, Rd & Pr 499; NP 1283

OR: Our Lady of Mount Carmel (1538)
From Com of BVM 1614
OOR 1061, Rd 499 & 1538, Pr 1540
MP 1626, Ps 1066, Ant & Pr 1540; DP 1071
EP 1634, Ps 1077, Ant & Pr 1540; NP 1283

17. Fri. Friday of the 15th Week in Ordinary Time
ALL 1082, Rd & Pr 504; NP 1285

18. Sat. Saturday of the 15th Week in Ordinary Time
ALL 1103, Rd & Pr 509; EP see below

OR: St. Camillus de Lellis, P (1533) **[transferred from 7/14]**
From Com of HM (Underpriv) 1866
OOR 1103, Rd 509 & 1533, Pr 1535
MP 1815, Ps 1108, Ant 1869, Pr 1535; DP 1112
EP see below

OR: BVM on Saturday—1642 & 1103
Rd 509 & 1642f, Pr 1653f; DP 1112
EP I (of Sunday) 1117, Ant & Pr 514; NP 1269

19. **Sun. SIXTEENTH SUNDAY IN ORDINARY TIME**
ALL 1122, Rd, Te Deum, Ant & Pr 514; NP 1272

20. Mon. Monday of the 16th Week in Ordinary Time
ALL 1143, Rd & Pr 518; NP 1275

OR: St. Apollinarius, B & M (*New*)
From Com of M 1707 or Pas 1734
OOR 1144, Rd 518 & 1712f, Pr 1719 or 1752
MP from Com, Ps 1148, Pr 1719 or 1752; DP 1154
EP from Com, Ps 1160, Pr 1719 or 1752; NP 1275

21. Tue. Tuesday of the 16th Week in Ordinary Time
ALL 1165, Rd & Pr 522; NP 1278

OR: St. Lawrence of Brindisi, P & D (1540)
From Com of Pas 1734 or D 1763
OOR 1166, Rd 522 & 1541, Pr 1542
MP from Com, Ps 1170, Pr 1542; DP 1176
EP from Com, Ps 1181, Pr 1542; NP 1278

22. Wed. St. Mary Magdalene (Mem) (1543)
From Com of HW 1835
OCR 1188, Rd 526 & 1543, Pr 1546
MP Hymn 1843, Ant 1545 & Ps 688, Rd, etc. 1545; DP 1197
EP Hymn 1849, Ant 1546 & Ps 1850, Rd, etc. 1547; NP 1280

23. Thu. Thursday of the 16th Week in Ordinary Time
ALL 1210, Rd & Pr 529; NP 1283

OR: St. Bridget, Rel (1547)
From Com of Rel 1858
OOR 1211, Rd 529 & 1548, Pr 1550
MP 1862, Ps 1214, Pr 1550; DP 1219
EP 1864, Ps 1225, Pr 1550; NP 1283

24. Fri. Friday of the 16th Week in Ordinary Time
ALL 1230, Rd & Pr 533; NP 1285

OR: St. Sharbel Makhlūf, P (*New*)
From Com of Pas 1734
OOR 1231, Rd 533 & 1738, Pr 1753
MP from Com, Ps 1234, Pr 1753; DP 1240
EP from Com, Ps 1246, Pr 1753; NP 1285

25. Sat. ST. JAMES, AP (F) (1551)
From Com of Ap 1659 and proper, Te Deum
DP 1259, Rd, etc. 1668, Pr 1554
EP I (of Sunday) 677, Ant & Pr 541; NP 1269

26. **Sun. SEVENTEENTH SUNDAY OF ORDINARY TIME**
ALL 682, Rd, Te Deum, Ant & Pr 541; NP 1272

27. Mon. Monday of the 17th Week in Ordinary Time
ALL 702, Rd & Pr 545; NP 1275

28. Tue. Tuesday of the 17th Week in Ordinary Time
ALL 722, Rd & Pr 549; NP 1278

29. Wed. St. Martha (Mem) (1559)
From Com of HW 1835
OOR 745, Rd 553 & 1560, Pr 1562

MP Hymn 1843, Ps 749, Ant & Pr 1562; DP 754
EP Hymn 1849, Ps 759, Ant & Pr 1562; NP 1280

30. Thu. Thursday of the 17th Week in Ordinary Time
ALL 765, Rd & Pr 558; NP 1283

OR: St. Peter Chrysologus, B & D (1562)
From Com of Pas 1734 or D 1763
OOR 765, Rd 558 & 1563, Pr 1564
MP from Com, Ps 769, Pr 1564; DP 774
EP from Com, Ps 780, Pr 1564; NP 1283

31. Fri. St. Ignatius of Loyola, P (Mem) (1565)
From Com of Pas 1734 or Rel 1858
OOR 786, Rd 562 & 1565, Pr 1567
MP from Com, Ps 790, Ant & Pr 1567; DP 796
EP from Com, Ps 802, Ant & Pr 1567; NP 1285

AUGUST

1. Sat. St. Alphonsus Liguori, B & D (Mem) (1568)
From Com of Pas 1734 or D 1763
OOR 807, Rd 566 & 1568, Pr 1569
MP from Com, Ps 811, Pr 1569; DP 816
EP see next volume (IV)

BEGIN VOLUME IV

EP I (of Sunday) 785, Ant & Pr 53; NP 1233

2. **Sun. EIGHTEENTH SUNDAY IN ORDINARY TIME**
ALL 790, Rd, Te Deum, Ant & Pr 53; NP 1236

3. Mon. Monday of the 18th Week in Ordinary Time
ALL 811, Rd and Pr 59; NP 1239

4. Tue. St. John Vianney, P (Mem) (1268)
From Com of Pas 1748
OOR 834, Rd 63 & 1269, Pr 1271
MP 1763, Ps 839, Pr 1271; DP 845
EP 1769, Ps 850, Pr 1271; NP 1242

5. Wed. Wednesday of the 18th Week in Ordinary Time
ALL 855, Rd & Pr 68; NP 1244

OR: Dedication of St. Mary Major (1271)
From Com of BVM 1628

OOR 856, Rd 68 & 1271, Pr 1273
MP 1640, Ps 861, Ant & Pr 1273; DP 867
EP 1648, Ps 874, Ant & Pr 1274; NP 1244

6. Thu. TRANSFIGURATION (F)
ALL 1278, Te Deum; DP Ps 890; EP 1291; NP 1247

7. Fri. Friday of the 18th Week in Ordinary Time
ALL 901, Rd & Pr 78; NP 1249

OR: St. Sixtus II, Po & Comps, Mm (1296)
From Com of Mm 1694
OOR 902, Rd 78 & 1296, Pr 1298
MP 1702, Ps 905, Pr 1298; DP 910
EP 1708, Ps 916, Pr 1298; NP 1249

OR: St. Cajetan, P (1299)
From Com of Pas 1748 or Rel 1872
OOR 902, Rd 78 & 1299, Pr 1301
MP from Com, Ps 905, Pr 1301; DP 910
EP from Com, Ps 916, Pr 1301; NP 1249

8. Sat. St. Dominic, P (Mem) (1301)
From Com of Pas 1748 or Rel 1872
OOR 923, Rd 83 & 1301, Pr 1303
MP from Com, Ps 926, Pr 1303; DP 932
EP I (of Sunday) 937, Ant & Pr 88; NP 1233

9. **Sun. NINETEENTH SUNDAY IN ORDINARY TIME**
ALL 942, Rd, Te Deum, Ant & Pr 88; NP 1236

10. Mon. ST. LAWRENCE, DE & M (F) (1303)
From Com of M 1721 and proper, Te Deum
DP 971, Rd, etc. 1734, Pr 1308; NP 1239

11. Tue. St. Clare, V (Mem) (1310)
From Com of V 1791 or Rel 1872
OOR 983, Rd 96 & 1310, Pr 1312
MP from Com, Ps 988, Pr 1312; DP 993
EP from Com, Ps 998, Pr 1312; NP 1242

12. Wed. Wednesday of the 19th Week in Ordinary Time
ALL 1003, Rd & Pr 101; NP 1244

OR: St. Jane Frances de Chantal, Rel (**New**) (14) or see Vol. I, 1240
From Com of Rel 1872 **[transferred from 8/18]**
OOR 1004, Rd 101 & (15), Pr (17)

MP 1876, Ps 1009, Pr (17); DP 1014
EP 1878, Ps 1020, Pr (17); NP 1244

13. Thu. Thursday of the 19th Week in Ordinary Time
ALL 1025, Rd & Pr 104; NP 1247

OR: Sts. Pontian, Po & M & Hippolytus, P & M (1312)
From Com of Mm 1694 or Pas 1748
OOR 1025, Rd 104 & 1313, Pr 1315
MP from Com, Ps 1030, Pr 1315; DP 1035
EP from Com, Ps 1041, Pr 1315; NP 1247

14. Fri. St. Maximilian Mary Kolbe, P & M (Mem) (**New**) (10)
From Com of Pas 1748 or M 1721
OOR 1046, Rd 108 & proper (11) or 1759 or 1726, Pr proper (10) or 1767 or 1733
MP from Com, Ps 1051, Ant & Pr proper (14) or as above
DP 1056; EP I (of Assumption) 1315; NP 1233

15. **Sat. ASSUMPTION OF BVM (Sol)** (not a holyday of obligation)
ALL 1318, Te Deum; DP Ps 1255; EP 1326; NP 1236

16. **Sun. TWENTIETH SUNDAY IN ORDINARY TIME**
ALL 1086, Rd, Te Deum, Ant & Pr 118; NP 1236

17. Mon. Monday of the 20th Week in Ordinary Time
ALL 1107, Rd & Pr 123; NP 1239

18. Tue. Tuesday of the 20th Week in Ordinary Time
ALL 1129, Rd & Pr 128; NP 1242

19. Wed. Wednesday of the 20th Week in Ordinary Time
ALL 1151, Rd & Pr 131; NP 1244

OR: St. John Eudes, P (1330)
From Com of Pas 1748 or Rel 1872
OOR 1152, Rd 131 & 1331, Pr 1332
MP from Com, Ps 1156, Pr 1332; DP 1161
EP from Com, Ps 1168, Pr 1332; NP 1244

20. Thu. St. Bernard, Ab & D (Mem) (1333)
From Com of D 1777 or Rel 1872
OOR 1175, Rd 136 & 1333, Pr 1335
MP from Com, Ps 1178, Ant & Pr 1335; DP 1183
EP from Com, Ps 1189, Ant & Pr 1335; NP 1247

21. Fri. St. Pius X, Po (Mem) (1335)
From Com of Po 1748
OOR 1195, Rd 140 & 1336, Pr 1338
MP 1763, Ps 1198, Pr 1338; DP 1204
EP 1769, Ps 1210, Pr 1338; NP 1249

22. Sat. Queenship of Mary (Mem) (1338)
From Com of BVM 1628
OOR 1215, Rd 145 & 1338, Pr 1341
MP 1640, Ps 1218, Ant & Pr 1340; DP 1223
EP I (of Sunday) 641, Ant & Pr 150; NP 1233

23. **Sun. TWENTY-FIRST SUNDAY IN ORDINARY TIME**
ALL 646, Rd, Te Deum, Ant & Pr 150; NP 1236

24. Mon. ST. BARTHOLOMEW, AP (F) (1344)
From Com of Ap 1673 and proper, Te Deum
DP 675, Rd, etc. 1682, Pr 1346; NP 1239

25. Tue. Tuesday of the 21st Week in Ordinary Time
ALL 686, Rd & Pr 160; NP 1242

OR: St. Louis (1347)
From Com of HM 1818
OOR 687, Rd 160 & 1347, Pr 1349
MP 1829, Ps 692, Pr 1349; DP 697
EP 1837, Ps 703, Pr 1349; NP 1242

OR: St. Joseph Calasanz, P (1349)
From Com of Tea 1885 or Pas 1748
OOR 687, Rd 160 & 1349, Pr 1351
MP from Com, Ps 692, Pr 1351; DP 697
EP from Com, Ps 703, Pr 1351; NP 1242

26. Wed. Wednesday of the 21st Week in Ordinary Time
ALL 708, Rd & Pr 164; NP 1244

27. Thu. St. Monica (Mem) (1352)
From Com of HW 1849
OOR 729, Rd 170 & 1352, Pr 1354
MP 1857, Ps 733, Ant & Pr 1354; DP 738
EP 1863, Ps 744, Ant & Pr 1354; NP 1247

28. Fri. St. Augustine, B & D (Mem) (1355)
From Com of Pas 1748 or D 1777
OOR 750, Rd 175 & 1355, Pr 1357

MP from Com, Ps 754, Ant & Pr 1357; DP 760
EP from Com, Ps 766, Ant 1358, Pr 1357; NP 1249

29. Sat. Beheading of St. John the Baptist, M (Mem) (1358)
From Com of M 1721
OOR 771, Rd 180 & 1358, Pr 1362
MP Hymn 1729, Ant 1360 & Ps 775, Rd, etc. 1361; DP 780
EP I (of Sunday) 785, Ant & Pr 185; NP 1233

30. **Sun. TWENTY-SECOND SUNDAY IN ORDINARY TIME**
ALL 790, Rd, Te Deum, Ant & Pr 185; NP 1236

31. Mon. Monday of the 22nd Week in Ordinary Time
ALL 811, Rd & Pr 191; NP 1239

SEPTEMBER

1. Tue. Tuesday of the 22nd Week in Ordinary Time
ALL 833, Rd & Pr 195; NP 1242

2. Wed. Wednesday of the 22nd Week in Ordinary Time
ALL 855, Rd & Pr 199; NP 1244

3. Thu. St. Gregory the Great, Po & D (Mem) (1365)
From Com of Pas 1748 or D 1777
OOR 881, Rd 204 & 1365, Pr 1367
MP from Com, Ps 884, Ant & Pr 1367; DP 890
EP from Com, Ps 896, Ant & Pr 1367; NP 1247

4. Fri. Friday of the 22nd Week in Ordinary Time
ALL 901, Rd & Pr 208; NP 1249

5. Sat. Saturday of the 22nd Week in Ordinary Time
ALL 922, Rd & Pr 213; EP see below

OR: BVM on Saturday—1656 & 923
Rd 213 & 1656f, Pr 1667f; DP 932
EP I (of Sunday) 937, Ant & Pr 218; NP 1233

6. **Sun. TWENTY-THIRD SUNDAY IN ORDINARY TIME**
ALL 942, Rd, Te Deum, Ant & Pr 218; NP 1236

7. Mon. Monday of the 23rd Week in Ordinary Time
ALL 962, Rd & Pr 223; NP 1239

8. Tue. BIRTH OF MARY (F) (1368)
From Com of BVM 1628 and proper, Te Deum
DP 993, Rd, etc. 1373; NP 1242

9. Wed. St. Peter Claver, P (Mem) (2016)
From Com of Pas 1748 or HM (Underpriv) 1880
OOR 1004, Rd 232 & 2016, Pr 2019
MP from Com, Ps 1009, Pr 2019; DP 1014
EP from Com, Ps 1020, Pr 2019; NP 1244

10. Thu. Thursday of the 23rd Week in Ordinary Time
ALL 1025, Rd & Pr 237; NP 1247

11. Fri. Friday of the 23rd Week in Ordinary Time
ALL 1046, Rd & Pr 243; NP 1249

12. Sat. Saturday of the 23rd Week in Ordinary Time
ALL 1067, Rd & Pr 248; EP see below

OR: The Most Holy Name of Mary (*New*)
From the Com of BVM 1628
OOR 1067, Rd 248 & 1635f, Pr 1645
MP 1640, Ps 1072, Pr 1645; DP 1076
EP see below

OR: BVM on Saturday—1656 & 1067
Rd 248 & 1656f, Pr 1667f; DP 1076
EP I (of Sunday) 1081, Ant & Pr 252; NP 1233

13. **Sun. TWENTY-FOURTH SUNDAY IN ORDINARY TIME**
ALL 1086, Rd, Te Deum, Ant & Pr 252; NP 1236

14. Mon. TRIUMPH OF THE CROSS (F)
ALL 1384, Te Deum; DP Ps 1118; EP 1396; NP 1239

15. Tue. Our Lady of Sorrows (Mem) (1401)
From Com of BVM 1628
OOR 1130, Rd 260 & 1401, Pr 1404
MP Hymn 1640, Ant 1403 & Ps 652, Rd, etc. 1403; DP 1140
EP 1648, Ant 1404 & Ps 1649, Rd, etc. 1404; NP 1242

16. Wed. Sts. Cornelius, Po & M & Cyprian, B & M (Mem) (1406)
From Com of Mm 1694 or Pas 1748
OOR 1152, Rd 265 & 1406, Pr 1410
MP from Com, Ps 1156, Ant & Pr 1410; DP 1161
EP from Com, Ps 1168, Ant 1411, Pr 1410; NP 1244

17. Thu. Thursday of the 24th Week in Ordinary Time
ALL 1174, Rd & Pr 269; NP 1247

OR: St. Robert Bellarmine, B & D (1411)
From Com of Pas 1748 or D 1777
OOR 1175, Rd 269 & 1411, Pr 1413
MP from Com, Ps 1178, Pr 1413; DP 1183
EP from Com, Ps 1189, Pr 1413; NP 1247

18. Fri. Friday of the 24th Week in Ordinary Time
ALL 1194, Rd & Pr 273; NP 1249

19. Sat. Saturday of the 24th Week in Ordinary Time
ALL 1214, Rd & Pr 278; EP see below

OR: St. Januarius, B & M (1413)
From Com of M 1721 or Pas 1748
OOR 1215, Rd 278 & 1414, Pr 1416
MP from Com, Ps 1218, Pr 1416; DP 1223
EP see below

OR: BVM on Saturday—1656 & 1215
Rd 278 & 1656f, Pr 1667f; DP 1223
EP I (of Sunday) 641, Ant & Pr 283; NP 1233

20. **Sun. TWENTY-FIFTH SUNDAY IN ORDINARY TIME**
ALL 646, Rd, Te Deum, Ant & Pr 283; NP 1236

21. Mon. ST. MATTHEW, AP & EVANGELIST (F) (1416)
From Com of Ap 1673 and proper, Te Deum
DP 675, Rd, etc. 1682, Pr 1420; NP 1239

22. Tue. Tuesday of the 25th Week in Ordinary Time
ALL 686, Rd & Pr 292; NP 1242

23. Wed. St. Pius of Pietrelcina, P (Mem) (*New*)
From Com of Pas 1748
OOR 709, Rd 296 & 1759, Pr 1767
MP from Com, Ps 713, Pr 1767; DP 718
EP from Com, Ps 723, Pr 1775; NP 1244

24. Thu. Thursday of the 25th Week in Ordinary Time
ALL 729, Rd & Pr 300; NP 1247

25. Fri. Friday of the 25th Week in Ordinary Time
ALL 750, Rd & Pr 304; NP 1249

26. Sat. Saturday of the 25th Week in Ordinary Time
ALL 771, Rd & Pr 309; EP see below

OR: Sts. Cosmas & Damian, Mm (1421)
From Com of Mm 1694
OOR 771, Rd 309 & 1421, Pr 1423
MP 1702, Ps 775, Pr 1423; DP 780
EP see below

OR: BVM on Saturday—1656 & 771
Rd 309 & 1656f, Pr 1667f; DP 780
EP I (of Sunday) 785, Ant & Pr 313; NP 1233

27. **Sun. TWENTY-SIXTH SUNDAY IN ORDINARY TIME**
ALL 790, Rd, Te Deum, Ant & Pr 313; NP 1236

28. Mon. Monday of the 26th Week in Ordinary Time
ALL 811, Rd & Pr 317; NP 1239

OR: St. Wenceslaus, M (1426)
From Com of M 1721
OOR 812, Rd 317 & 1427, Pr 1428
MP 1729, Ps 817, Pr 1428; DP 822
EP 1735, Ps 828, Pr 1428; NP 1239

OR: St. Lawrence Ruiz & Comps, Mm (**New**) (21)
From Com of Mm 1694
OOR 812, Rd 317 & proper (22) or 1700, Pr proper (24) or 1706
MP 1702, Ps 817, Pr proper (24) or 1706; DP 822
EP 1708, Ps 828, Pr proper (24) or 1713; NP 1239

29. Tue. STS. MICHAEL, GABRIEL & RAPHAEL, ARCHANGELS (F)
ALL 1429, Te Deum; DP Ps 845; NP 1242

30. Wed St. Jerome, P & D (Mem) (1447)
From Com of D 1777
OOR 856, Rd 325 & 1447, Pr 1449
MP 1782, Ps 861, Ant 1783, Pr 1449; DP 867
EP 1784, Ps 874, Ant 1785, Pr 1449; NP 1244

OCTOBER

1. Thu. St. Theresa of the Child Jesus, V & D (Mem) (1450)
From Com of V 1791 or D 1777
OOR 881, Rd 329 & 1450, Pr 1452
MP from Com, Ps 884, Ant & Pr 1452; DP 890
EP from Com, Ps 896, Ant & Pr 1452; NP 1247

2. Fri. Guardian Angels (Mem) (1452)
OOR 1453, Ps 902, Rd 332 & 1453, Pr 1458
MP 1455, Ps 652, Rd, etc. 1456; DP 910, Rd, etc. 1458
EP 1459; NP 1249

3. Sat. Saturday of the 26th Week in Ordinary Time
ALL 922, Rd & Pr 336; EP see below

OR: BVM on Saturday—1656 & 923
Rd 336 & 1656f, Pr 1667f; DP 932
EP I (of Sunday) 937, Ant & Pr 340; NP 1233

4. **Sun. TWENTY-SEVENTH SUNDAY IN ORDINARY TIME**
ALL 942, Rd, Te Deum, Ant & Pr 340; NP 1236

5. Mon. Monday of the 27th Week in Ordinary Time
ALL 962, Rd & Pr 345; NP 1239

6. Tue. Tuesday of the 27th Week in Ordinary Time
ALL 982, Rd & Pr 349; NP 1242

OR: St. Bruno, P (1468)
From Com of Pas 1748 or Rel 1872
OOR 983, Rd 349 & 1468, Pr 1470
MP from Com, Ps 988, Pr 1470; DP 993
EP from Com, Ps 998, Pr 1470; NP 1242

OR: Bl. Marie Rose Durocher, V (**New**) (24)
From Com of V 1791
OOR 983, Rd 349 & 1796, Pr proper (25) or 1803
MP 1800, Ps 988, Pr proper (25) or 1803; DP 993
EP 1805, Ps 998, Pr proper (25) or 1805; NP 1242

7. Wed. Our Lady of the Rosary (Mem) (1470)
From Com of BVM 1628
OOR 1004, Rd 353 & 1470, Pr 1473
MP 1472, Ps 652; DP 1014
EP 1474, Ps 1649, Pr 1473; NP 1244

8. Thu. Thursday of the 27th Week in Ordinary Time
ALL 1025, Rd & Pr 357; NP 1247

9. Fri. Friday of the 27th Week in Ordinary Time
ALL 1046, Rd & Pr 362; NP 1249

OR: St. Denis, B & M & Comps, Mm (1475)
From Com of Mm 1694

OOR 1046, Rd 362 & 1475, Pr 1477
MP 1702, Ps 1051, Pr 1477; DP 1056
EP 1708, Ps 1062, Pr 1477; NP 1249

OR: St. John Leonardi, P (1477)
From Com of Pas 1748 or HM (Underpriv) 1880
OOR 1046, Rd 362 & 1478, Pr 1480
MP from Com, Ps 1051, Pr 1480; DP 1056
EP from Com, Ps 1062, Pr 1480; NP 1249

10. Sat. Saturday of the 27th Week in Ordinary Time
ALL 1067, Rd & Pr 366; EP see below

OR: BVM on Saturday—1656 & 1067
Rd 366 & 1656f, Pr 1667f; DP 1076
EP I (of Sunday) 1081, Ant & Pr 370; NP 1233

11. **Sun. TWENTY-EIGHTH SUNDAY IN ORDINARY TIME**
ALL 1086, Rd, Te Deum, Ant & Pr 370; NP 1236

12. Mon. Monday of the 28th Week in Ordinary Time
ALL 1107, Rd & Pr 376; NP 1239

13. Tue. Tuesday of the 28th Week in Ordinary Time
ALL 1129, Rd & Pr 380; NP 1242

14. Wed. Wednesday of the 28th Week in Ordinary Time
ALL 1151, Rd & Pr 384; NP 1244

OR: St. Callistus I, Po & M (1480)
From Com of M 1721 or Pas 1748
OOR 1152, Rd 384 & 1480, Pr 1482
MP from Com, Ps 1156, Pr 1482; DP 1161
EP from Com, Ps 1168, Pr 1482; NP 1244

15. Thu. St. Teresa of Avila, V & D (Mem) (1482)
From Com of V 1791 or D 1777
OOR 1175, Rd 389 & 1483, Pr 1484
MP from Com, Ps 1178, Pr 1484; DP 1183
EP from Com, Ps 1189, Pr 1484; NP 1247

16. Fri. Friday of the 28th Week in Ordinary Time
ALL 1194, Rd & Pr 394; NP 1249

OR: St. Hedwig, Rel (1485)
From Com of HW (Underpriv) 1880 or Rel 1872
OOR 1195, Rd 394 & 1485, Pr 1487

MP from Com, Ps 1198, Pr 1487; DP 1204
EP from Com, Ps 1210, Pr 1487; NP 1249

OR: St. Margaret Mary Alacoque, V (1487)
From Com of V 1791 or Rel 1872
OOR 1195, Rd 394 & 1487, Pr 1489
MP from Com, Ps 1198, Pr 1489; DP 1204
EP from Com, Ps 1210, Pr 1489; NP 1249

17. Sat. St. Ignatius of Antioch, B & M (Mem) (1490)
From Com of M 1721 or Pas 1748
OOR 1215, Rd 399 & 1490, Pr 1492
MP from Com, Ps 1218, Ant & Pr 1492; DP 1223
EP I (of Sunday) 641, Ant & Pr 405; NP 1233

18. **Sun. TWENTY-NINTH SUNDAY IN ORDINARY TIME**
ALL 646, Rd, Te Deum, Ant & Pr 405; NP 1236

19. Mon. Sts. Isaac Jogues & John de Brebeuf, Pp & Mm & Comps, Mm (Mem) (2019)
From the Com of Mm 1694 or Pas 1748
OOR 666, Rd 410 & 2020, Pr 2021
MP from Com, Ps 670, Pr 2021; DP 675
EP from Com, Ps 681, Pr 2021; NP 1239

20. Tue. Tuesday of the 29th Week in Ordinary Time
ALL 686, Rd & Pr 414; NP 1242

OR: St. Paul of the Cross, P (1505) **[transferred from 10/19]**
From Com of Pas 1748 or Rel 1872
OOR 687, Rd 414 & 1505, Pr 1507
MP from Com, Ps 692, Pr 1507; DP 697
EP from Com, Ps 703, Pr 1507; NP 1242

21. Wed. Wednesday of the 29th Week in Ordinary Time
ALL 708, Rd & Pr 419; NP 1244

22. Thu. Thursday of the 29th Week in Ordinary Time
ALL 729, Rd & Pr 423; NP 1247

OR: St. John Paul II, Po (*New*)
From the Com of Pas 1748
OOR 729, Rd 423 & 1754, Pr 1766
MP 1763, Ps 733, Pr 1766; DP 738
EP 1769, Ps 744, Pr 1744; NP 1247

23. Fr . Friday of the 29th Week in Ordinary Time
ALL 750, Rd & Pr 427; NP 1249

OR: St John of Capistrano, P (1507)
From Com of Pas 1748
OOR 750, Rd 427 & 1507, Pr 1509
MP 1763, Ps 754, Pr 1509; DP 760
EP 1769, Ps 766, Pr 1509; NP 1249

24. Sat. Saturday of the 29th Week in Ordinary Time
ALL 771, Rd & Pr 431; EP see below

OR: St. Anthony Claret, B (1510)
From Com of Pas 1748
OOR 771, Rd 431 & 1510, Pr 1511
MP 1763, Ps 775, Pr 1511; DP 780
EP see below

OR: BVM on Saturday—1656 & 771
Rd 431 & 1656f, Pr 1667f; DP 780
EP I (of Sunday) 785, Ant & Pr 437; NP 1233

25. **Sun. THIRTIETH SUNDAY IN ORDINARY TIME**
ALL 790, Rd, Te Deum, Ant & Pr 437; NP 1236

26. Mon. Monday of the 30th Week in Ordinary Time
ALL 811, Rd & Pr 441; NP 1239

27. Tue. Tuesday of the 30th Week in Ordinary Time
ALL 833, Rd & Pr 446; NP 1242

28. Wed. STS. SIMON & JUDE, AP (F) (1512)
From Com of Ap 1673 and proper, Te Deum
DP 367, Rd, etc. 1682, Pr 1514; NP 1244

29. Thu. Thursday of the 30th Week in Ordinary Time
ALL 880, Rd & Pr 454; NP 1247

30. Fri. Friday of the 30th Week in Ordinary Time
ALL 901, Rd & Pr 459; NP 1249

31. Sat. Saturday of the 30th Week in Ordinary Time
ALL 922, Rd & Pr 463; EP see below

OR: BVM on Saturday—1656 & 923
Rd 463 & 1656f, Pr 1667f; DP 932
EP I (of All Saints) 1515; NP 1233

NOVEMBER

1. **Sun. ALL SAINTS (Sol)**
ALL 1520, Te Deum; DP Ps 1255; NP 1236

2. Mon. ALL SOULS (1537)
From Office for the 1891 & proper; NP 1236

3. Tue. Tuesday of the 31st Week in Ordinary Time
ALL 982, Rd & Pr 477; NP 1242

OR: St. Martin de Porres, Rel (1540)
From Com of Rel 1872
OOR 983, Rd 477 & 1541, Pr 1543
MP 1876, Ps 988, Ant & Pr 1543; DP 993
EP 1878, Ps 998, Ant & Pr 1543; NP 1242

4. Wed. St. Charles Borromeo, B (Mem) (1543)
From Com of Pas 1748
OOR 1004, Rd 482 & 1544, Pr 1546
MP 1763, Ps 1009, Pr 1546; DP 1014
EP 1769, Ps 1020, Pr 1546; NP 1244

5. Thu. Thursday of the 31st Week in Ordinary Time
ALL 1025, Rd & Pr 486; NP 1247

6. Fri. Friday of the 31st Week in Ordinary Time
ALL 1046, Rd & Pr 491; NP 1249

7. Sat. Saturday of the 31st Week in Ordinary Time
ALL 1067, Rd & Pr 495; EP see below

OR: BVM on Saturday—1656 & 1067
Rd 495 & 1656f, Pr 1667f; DP 1076
EP I (of Sunday) 1081, Ant & Pr 500; NP 1233

8. **Sun. THIRTY-SECOND SUNDAY IN ORDINARY TIME**
ALL 1086, Rd, Te Deum, Ant & Pr 500; NP 1236

9. Mon. DEDICATION OF ST. JOHN LATERAN (F) (1546)
From Com of Ded 1600 and proper, Te Deum
DP 1118, Rd, etc. 1612, Pr 1611; EP 1614; NP 1239

10. Tue. St. Leo the Great, Po & D (Mem) (1548)
From Com of Pas 1748 or D 1777
OOR 1130, Rd 510 & 1549, Pr 1551
MP from Com, Ps 1134, Pr 1551; DP 1140
EP from Com, Ps 1145, Pr 1551; NP 1242

11. Wed. St. Martin of Tours, B (Mem) (1551)
From Com of Pas 1748
OOR 1152, Rd 514 & 1552, Pr 1555
MP Hymn 1763, Ant 1554 & Ps 652, Rd, etc. 1554; DP 1161
EP Hymn 1769, Ant 1555, Ps 1770, Rd, etc. 1555; NP 1244

12. Thu. St. Josaphat, B & M (Mem) (1556)
From Com of M 1721 or Pas 1748
OOR 1175, Rd 518 & 1557, Pr 1558
MP from Com, Ps 1178, Pr 1558; DP 1183
EP from Com, Ps 1189, Pr 1558; NP 1247

13. Fri. St. Frances Xavier Cabrini, V (Mem) (2022)
From Com of V 1791 or HW (Underpriv) 1880 or Rel 1872
OOR 1195, Rd 523 & 2022, Pr 2024
MP from Com, Ps 1198, Pr 2024; DP 1204
EP from Com, Ps 1210, Pr 2024; NP 1249

14. Sat. Saturday of the 32nd Week in Ordinary Time
ALL 1214, Rd & Pr 527; EP see below

OR: BVM on Saturday—1656 & 1215
Rd 527 & 1656f, Pr 1667f; DP 1223
EP I (of Sunday) 641, Ant & Pr 532; NP 1233

15. **Sun. THIRTY-THIRD SUNDAY IN ORDINARY TIME**
ALL 646, Rd, Te Deum, Ant & Pr 532; NP 1236

16. Mon. Monday of the 33rd Week in Ordinary Time
ALL 666, Rd & Pr 538; NP 1239

OR: St. Margaret of Scotland (1561)
From Com of HW (Underpriv) 1880
OOR 666, Rd 538 & 1562, Pr 1563
MP 1857, Ps 670, Ant 1883, Pr 1563; DP 675
EP 1863, Ps 681, Ant 1884, Pr 1563; NP 1239

OR: St. Gertrude, V (1564)
From Com of V 1791 or Rel 1872
OOR 666, Rd 538 & 1564, Pr 1566
MP from Com, Ps 670, Pr 1566; DP 675
EP from Com, 681, Pr 1566; NP 1239

17. Tue. St. Elizabeth of Hungary, Rel (Mem) (1567)
From Com of HW (Underpriv) 1880
OOR 687, Rd 542 & 1567, Pr 1569

MP 1857, Ps 692, Ant 1883, Pr 1569; DP 697
EP 1863, Ps 703, Ant 1884, Pr 1569; NP 1242

18. Wed. Wednesday of the 33rd Week in Ordinary Time
ALL 708, Rd & Pr 548; NP 1244

OR: Dedication of the Churches of Sts. Peter & Paul, Ap (1569)
From Com of Ap 1673
OOR 709, Rd 548 & 1570, Pr 1571
MP 1680, Ps 713, Ant & Pr 1571; DP 718
EP 1683, Ps 723, Ant 1572 & Pr 1571; NP 1244

OR: St. Rose Philippine Duchesne, V (**New**) (26)
From Com of V 1791
OOR 709, Rd 548 & 1796, Pr proper (26) or 1803
MP 1800, Ps 713, Pr proper (26) or 1803; DP 718
EP 1805, Ps 723, Pr proper (26) or 1811; NP 1244

19. Thu. Thursday of the 33rd Week in Ordinary Time
ALL 729, Rd & Pr 552; NP 1247

20. Fri. Friday of the 33rd Week in Ordinary Time
ALL 750, Rd & Pr 557; NP 1249

21. Sat. Presentation of Mary (Mem) (1572)
From Com of BVM 1628
OOR 771, Rd 561 & 1572, Pr 1575
MP 1640, Ps 775, Ant & Pr 1575; DP 780
EP I (of Christ the King) 566; NP 1233

22. **Sun. CHRIST THE KING (Sol)**
ALL 570, Te Deum; DP 657; NP 1236

23. Mon. Monday of the 34th Week in Ordinary Time
ALL 811, Rd & Pr 587; NP 1239

OR: St. Clement I, Po & M (1578)
From Com of M 1721 or Pas 1748
OOR 812, Rd 587 & 1579, Pr 1580
MP from Com, Ps 817, Pr 1580; DP 822
EP from Com, Ps 828, Pr 1580; NP 1239

OR: St. Columban, Ab (1581)
From Com of Pas 1748 or Rel 1872
OOR 812, Rd 587 & 1581, Pr 1583
MP from Com, Ps 817, Pr 1583; DP 822
EP from Com, Ps 828, Pr 1583; NP 1239

OR: Bl. Miguel Agustín Pro, P & M (**New**) (27)
From Com of M 1721 or Pas 1748
OOR 812, Rd 587 & Pr proper (28) or 1726 or 1752, Pr proper (28) or 1733 or 1767
MP from Com, Ps 817, Pr as above; DP 822
EP from Com, Ps 828, Pr as above; NP 1239

24. Tue. St. Andrew Dung-Lac, P & Comps, Mm (Mem) (**New**) (28)
From Com of Mm 1694
OOR 834, Rd 590 & (29), Pr proper (31) or 1706
MP 1702, Ps 839, Pr proper (31) or 1706; DP 845
EP 1708, Ps 850; Pr proper (31) or 1713; NP 1242

25. Wed. Wednesday of the 34th Week in Ordinary Time
ALL 855, Rd & Pr 594; NP 1244

OR: St. Catherine of Alexandria, V & M (*New*)
From Com of M 1721 or V 1791
OOR 856, Rd 594 & 1721 or 1803, Pr 1790
MP from Com, Ps 861, Pr 1803; DP 867
EP from Com, Ps 874, Pr 1811; NP 1244

26. Thu. Thursday of the 34th Week in Ordinary Time **(Thanksgiving Day)**
ALL 880, Rd & Pr 597; NP 1247

27. Fri. Friday of the 34th Week in Ordinary Time
ALL 901, Rd & Pr 601; NP 1249

28. Sat. Saturday of the 34th Week in Ordinary Time
ALL 922, Rd & Pr 606; EP see next volume (I)

OR: BVM on Saturday—1656 & 923
Rd 606 & 1656f, Pr 1667f; DP 932; EP see next volume (I)

BEGIN VOLUME I

EP I (of Sunday) 137, Hymn 126 or 677, Ps 678; NP 1169

29. **Sun. FIRST SUNDAY OF ADVENT**
OOR 139, Hymn 121 or 682, Ps 683, Te Deum, Pr 146
MP 144, Hymn 122 or 687, Ps 687
DP 691, Ant, etc. 146
EP II 148, Hymn 126 or 694, Ps 695; NP 1172

30. Mon. ST. ANDREW, AP (F) (1201)
From Com of Ap 1354 and proper, Te Deum
DP 707, Ant 155, Rd, etc. 1363, Pr 1207; NP 1175

DECEMBER

1. Tue. Tuesday of the 1st Week of Advent
ALL 714, Ant, Rd, etc. 158; NP 1178

2. Wed. Wednesday of the 1st Week of Advent
ALL 732, Ant, Rd, etc. 167; NP 1180

3. Thu. St. Francis Xavier, P (Mem) (1210)
From Com of Pas 1428
OOR 1428, Ps 749, Rd 175 & 1210, Pr 1212
MP 1443, Ps 753, Pr 1212; DP 757, Ant, etc. 180
EP 1449, Ps 761, Pr 1212; NP 1183

4. Fri. Friday of the 1st Week of Advent
ALL 765, Ant, Rd, etc. 183; NP 1185

OR: St. John Damascene, P & D (1212)
From Com of D 1458
OOR 1458, Ps 765, Rd 183 & 1212, Pr 1214
MP 1464, Ps 769, Pr 1214; DP 773, Ant, etc. 187
EP 1466, Ps 777, Pr 1214; NP 1185

5. Sat. Saturday of the 1st Week of Advent
ALL 781, Ant, Rd, etc. 190, Pr 195
EP I (of Sunday) 197, Hymn 126 or 793, Ps 794; NP 1169

6. **Sun. SECOND SUNDAY OF ADVENT**
OOR 199, Hymn 121 or 798, Ps 798, Te Deum, Pr 205
MP 203, Hymn 122 or 802, Ps 804; DP 808, Ant, etc. 206
EP II 207, Hymn 126 or 811, Ps 811; NP 1172

7. Mon. St. Ambrose, B & D (Mem) (1217)
From Com of D 1458
OOR 1458, Ps 817, Rd 209 & 1218, Pr 1220
MP 1464, Ps 822, Pr 1220; DP 825, Ant, etc. 215
EP I (of Immaculate Conception); ALL 1221; NP 1175

8. **Tue. IMMACULATE CONCEPTION (Sol)** (holyday of obligation)
ALL 1224, Te Deum; DP Ps 1191; NP 1172

9. Wed. Wednesday of the 2nd Week of Advent
ALL 851, Ant, Rd, etc. 225; NP 1180

OR: St. Juan Diego (**New**) (32)
From Com of HM 1500
OOR 1500, Ps 852, Rd 225 & 1508, Pr proper (33) or 1516

MP 1512, Ps 857, Pr proper (33) or 1516
DP 862, Ant, Rd, etc. 230
EP 1519, Ps 867, Pr proper (33) or 1524; NP 1180

10. Thu. Thursday of the 2nd Week of Advent
ALL 872, Ant, Rd, etc. 233; NP 1183

11. Fri. Friday of the 2nd Week of Advent
ALL 890, Ant, Rd, etc. 242; NP 1185

OR: St. Damasus I, Po (1237)
From Com of Pas 1428
OOR 1428, Ps 891, Rd 242 & 1237, Pr 1239
MP 1443, Ps 894, Pr 1239; DP 898, Ant, etc. 247
EP 1449, Ps 902, Pr 1239; NP 1185

12. Sat. OUR LADY OF GUADALUPE (F) (**New**) (33)
From Com of BVM 1326 & proper; Invit (33)
OOR (34), Ps 1328, Rd (35), Te Deum, Pr (42)
MP (42), Ps 688, Pr (45); DP 916, Ant, etc. 1342
EP I (of Sunday) 256, Hymn 126 or 920, Ps 921; NP 1169

13. **Sun. THIRD SUNDAY OF ADVENT**
OOR Ant at Invit 258, Hymn 121 or 925, Ps 925, Rd & Responsories 259, Te Deum, Pr 264
MP 263, Hymn 122 or 928, Ps 929, Rd, Ant & Intercessions 264
DP Hymn 658, Ps 934, Ant, etc. 265
EP II 266, Hymn 126 or 937, Ps 937, Rd, Ant & Intercessions 266, Pr 268; NP 1172

14. Mon. St. John of the Cross, P & D (Mem) (1245)
From Com of D 1458
OOR 1458, Ps 941, Rd 269 & 1246, Pr 1247
MP 1464, Ps 945, Pr 1247; DP 949, Ant, etc. 274
EP 1466, Ps 953, Pr 1247; NP 1175

15. Tue. Tuesday of the 3rd Week of Advent
ALL 957, Ant, Rd, etc. 277; NP 1178

16. Wed. Wednesday of the 3rd Week of Advent
ALL 975, Ant, Rd, etc. 285; NP 1180

17. Thu. Thursday of the 3rd Week of Advent
ALL 994, Ant at Invit 647, Ant, Rd, etc. 318, Pr 323; NP 1183

18. Fri. Friday of the 3rd Week of Advent
ALL 1012, Ant, Rd, etc. 326, Pr 331; NP 1185

19. Sat. Saturday of the 3rd Week of Advent
ALL 1030, Ant, Rd, etc. 334, Pr 340
EP I (of Sunday) 309, Hymn 133 or 1042, Ps 1043
Ant at Mag 342; NP 1169

20. **Sun. FOURTH SUNDAY OF ADVENT**
OOR 311 & 343, Hymn 132 or 1047, Ps 1048, Te Deum, Pr 313
MP 312, Hymn 132 or 1051, Ps 1053; DP 1057, Ant, etc. 314
EP II 315, Hymn 133 or 1060, Ps 1060, Ant at Mag 350, Intercessions & Pr 316; NP 1172

21. Mon. Monday of the 4th Week of Advent
OOR 1064, Rd 351, Pr 356 (May add Rd of St. Peter Canisius, P & D with his Pr 1247-1249)
MP 1069, Rd, etc. 355 (May add Ant & Pr of St. Peter 1249)
DP 1074, Ant, Rd, etc. 356
EP 1077, Rd, etc. 358 (May add Ant & Pr of St. Peter 1250)
NP 1175

22. Tue. Tuesday of the 4th Week of Advent
ALL 1082, Ant, Rd, etc. 359, Pr 365; NP 1178

23. Wed. Wednesday of the 4th Week of Advent
OOR 1099, Rd 368, Pr 373 (May add Rd of St. John of Kanty, P with his Pr 1250-1252)
MP 1104, Rd 372 (May add Ant & Pr of St. John 1252)
DP 1109, Rd, etc. 374
EP 1112, Rd, etc. 375 (May add Ant & Pr of St. John 1252)
NP 1180

24. Thu. Thursday of the 4th Week of Advent
ALL 1118, Ant at Invit 376, Rd, etc. 377
MP 381, Ps 1122; DP 383, Ps 1127; EP I of Christmas ALL 394
NP 1169 (if not present at OOR & Midnight Mass)

25. **Fri. CHRISTMAS (Sol)**
OOR 399, Te Deum and Prayer 406 only if Mass does not follow; if Mass follows, say the Gloria (without introductory rite[s]) followed by Opening Prayer [Collect] of Mass.
MP (Not after Midnight Mass, but in Morning) ALL 407
DP 409; EP 414; NP 1169 or 1172

26. Sat. ST. STEPHEN, FIRST MARTYR (F) (1253)
From Com of M 1401 and Proper; Te Deum

DP 1160, Rd, etc. 1260, Pr 1259
EP I (of Holy Family) 421; NP 1169 or 1172

27. **Sun. HOLY FAMILY (F) (424)**
From Com of BVM 1326 & Proper; Te Deum
DP 691, Hymn 385, Ant, Rd, etc. 431
EP II 432; NP 1169 or 1172

28. Mon. HOLY INNOCENTS, Mm (F) (1272)
From Com of Mm 1375 and Proper; Te Deum
DP 707, Ant, Rd, etc. 1277, Pr 1277
EP 414, Rd, etc. 440; NP 1169 or 1172

29. Tue. FIFTH DAY IN THE OCTAVE OF CHRISTMAS
COR 442, Te Deum, Pr 450 (May add Rd of St. Thomas Becket, B & M with his Pr 1279-1281)
MP 407, Rd, etc. 448 (May add Ant & Pr of St. Thomas 1281)
DP 725, Ant, Rd, etc. 450
EP 414, Rd, etc. 451 (May add Ant & Pr of St. Thomas 1282)
NP 1169 or 1172

30. Wed. SIXTH DAY IN THE OCTAVE OF CHRISTMAS
OOR 454, Te Deum, Pr 462
MP 407, Rd, etc. 461; DP 741, Ant, Rd, etc. 463
EP 414, Rd, etc. 464; NP 1169 or 1172

31. Thu. SEVENTH DAY IN THE OCTAVE OF CHRISTMAS
OOR 466, Te Deum, Pr 474 (May add Rd of St. Sylvester I, Po with his Pr 1282-1284)
MP 407, Rd, etc. 473 (May add Ant & Pr of St. Sylvester 1284)
DP 757, Ant, Rd, etc. 474
EP I (of Mary) 476; NP 1169

The
LITURGY OF THE HOURS
is truly the prayer of the Church
for all the people of God —
bishops, priests, deacons,
religious and the
laity.

ISBN 978-1-941243-10-7
9 781941 243107 90000

uide is No. 400/G

ISBN 978-1-941243-10-7